Communicating

IN THE DIGITAL WORLD

By
Anastasia
Suen

YOUR POSITIVE Digital Footprint

CRABTREE
PUBLISHING COMPANY
WWW.CRABTREEBOOKS.COM

Author: Anastasia Suen

Series research and development: Reagan Miller

Editors: Janine Deschenes, Reagan Miller,

Proofreader and indexer: Angela Kaelberer

Design, photo research, and prepress:
Margaret Amy Salter

Print coordinator: Katherine Berti

Photo Credits

blog.elanco.org p 24 (bottom right), screenshot 2018-04-20

All other images from Shutterstock

Library and Archives Canada Cataloguing in Publication

Suen, Anastasia, author
Communicating in the digital world / Anastasia Suen.

(Your positive digital footprint)
Includes index.
Issued in print and electronic formats.
ISBN 978-0-7787-4600-3 (hardcover).--
ISBN 978-0-7787-4604-1 (softcover).--
ISBN 978-1-4271-2044-1 (HTML)

1. Communication and technology--Juvenile literature. 2. Communication--Data processing--Juvenile literature. 3. Communication--Social aspects--Juvenile literature. 4. Information technology--Social aspects--Juvenile literature. 5. Internet--Social aspects--Juvenile literature. I. Title.

P96.T42S84 2018 j302.23'1 C2018-901263-3
C2018-901264-1

Library of Congress Cataloging-in-Publication Data

Names: Suen, Anastasia, author.
Title: Communicating in the digital world / Anastasia Suen.
Description: New York : Crabtree Publishing, [2018] |
Series: Your positive digital footprint | Includes index.
Identifiers: LCCN 2018012558 (print) | LCCN 2018013150 (ebook) |
ISBN 9781427120441 (Electronic) |
ISBN 9780778746003 (hardcover : alk. paper) |
ISBN 9780778746041 (pbk. : alk. paper)
Subjects: LCSH: Internet and children--Juvenile literature. | Information technology--Juvenile literature. | Telecommunication--Juvenile literature.
Classification: LCC HQ784.I58 (ebook) | LCC HQ784.I58 S84 2018 (print) | DDC 303.48/33--dc23
LC record available at https://lccn.loc.gov/2018012558

Crabtree Publishing Company

www.crabtreebooks.com 1-800-387-7650

Printed in the U.S.A./052018/BG20180327

Published in Canada
Crabtree Publishing
616 Welland Ave.
St. Catharines, Ontario
L2M 5V6

Published in the United States
Crabtree Publishing
PMB 59051
350 Fifth Avenue, 59th Floor
New York, New York 10118

Published in the United Kingdom
Crabtree Publishing
Maritime House
Basin Road North, Hove
BN41 1WR

Published in Australia
Crabtree Publishing
3 Charles Street
Coburg North
VIC, 3058

Contents

Communicating: Then and Now 4
How do People Communicate? 6
The Goal of Communication 8
Lifelong Digital Citizen 10
Email 12
Sending Email 14
Clear Communication 16
Blogging 18
Starting Your Own Blog 20
Pages and Posts 22
Telling a Story 24
Visual Communication 26
Overcoming Communication Roadblocks 28
Glossary 30
Learning More 31
Index and About the Author 32

Communicating - Then and Now

You **communicate** every day in different ways. You communicate when you express your thoughts. You communicate when you share images with others. You even communicate without saying anything.

Flashback to 1978

If you could go back in time, you could see how much things have changed. To communicate with your friends a few decades ago, you had to find a phone. There might have been a phone on the wall in the kitchen. This phone with a curly cord could only take one call at a time.

If someone else was using the phone at home, you had to go somewhere else to make a call. You might have had to look for a payphone. These phones took coins to work! After you put in enough money to make the call, then you could dial the number.

When a payphone's money ran out, the call ended! How do you make phone calls today?

Flash Forward

Today you can call your friend from a phone that fits in your pocket. A smartphone can make a call to and from almost anywhere. But you know that's not all. You can use your smartphone to send a text message. An **emoji** or two can share what you are thinking or how you feel.

A smartphone also has a camera. You can snap a photo and send it to your friend. You can talk to friends with a video **app** like Skype or Facetime. You can share photos and videos instantly on Instagram and Snapchat.

The communication possibilities you hold in your pocket are endless! But with digital advancements come responsibilities, too. As a user of digital technology, you are also a **digital citizen**. This means you are part of a **digital community**—and you have a responsibility to contribute to it in a safe, positive, and meangingful way.

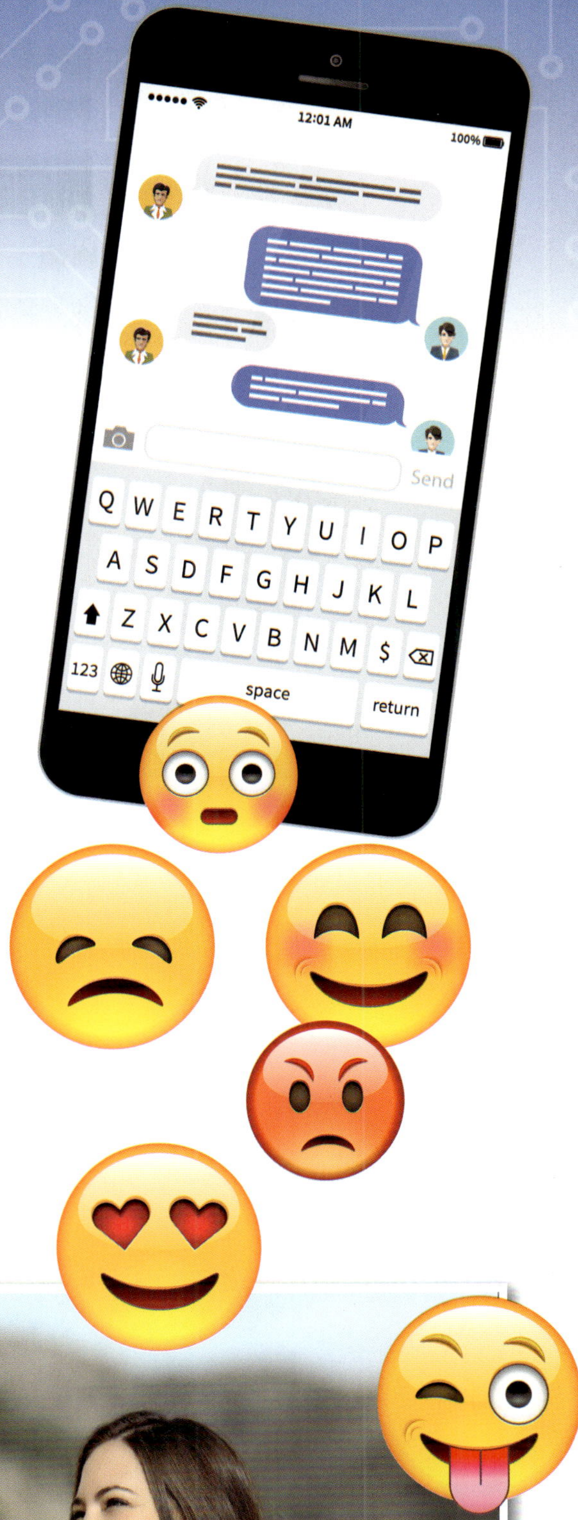

In 2018, you can communicate on a phone with spoken words, written words, and pictures.

How do People Communicate?

You can call and talk with your smartphone. You can send texts and images. You can share your thoughts and feelings. But that is only the beginning of the communication cycle. Someone needs to receive your message.

Communication requires both a sender and a receiver. When you communicate, you give something to someone else. When one person gives something, there needs to be someone else to receive it.

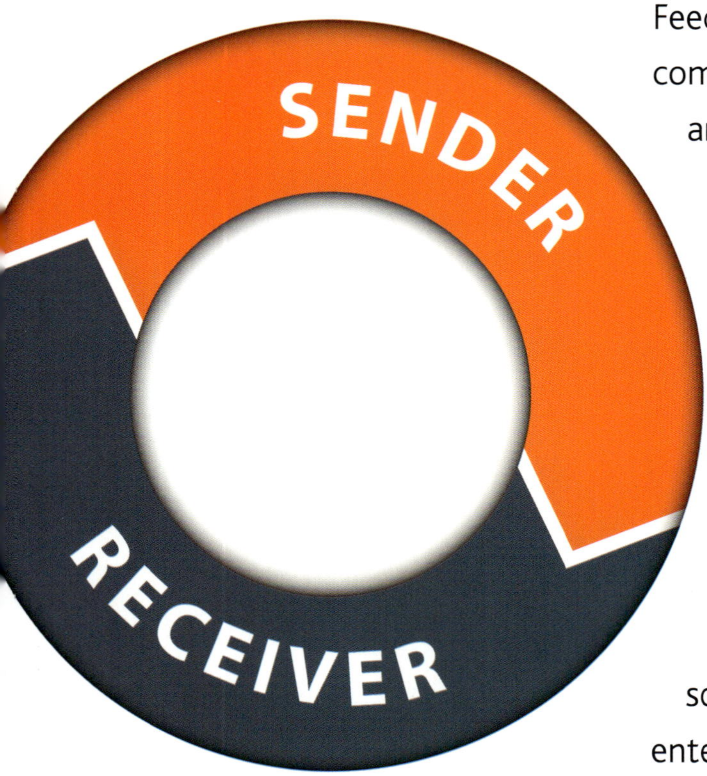

Feedback

Feedback is the response that keeps communication going. If your message is received and understood by the other person, they will respond. Now you are the one receiving the message. The other person will know that their message was received and understood when you respond.

People communicate to inform or tell others about something; to instruct someone on how to complete a task; to motivate someone to do something; to persuade or convince someone to think or feel a certain way; or to entertain someone.

Why People Communicate

Verb | **Face to Face** | **Digital Communication**

To inform:

"Mom, I have practice after school today."

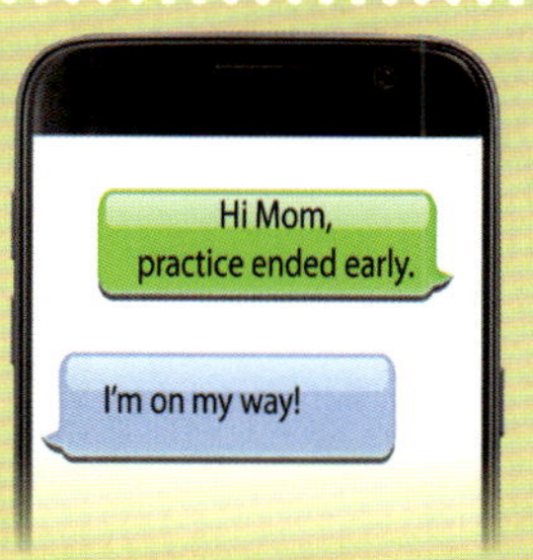

To instruct:

"Multiply these numbers."

To motivate:

"You guys are doing great!"

To entertain:

"Knock knock..."

To persuade:

"It will be fun!"

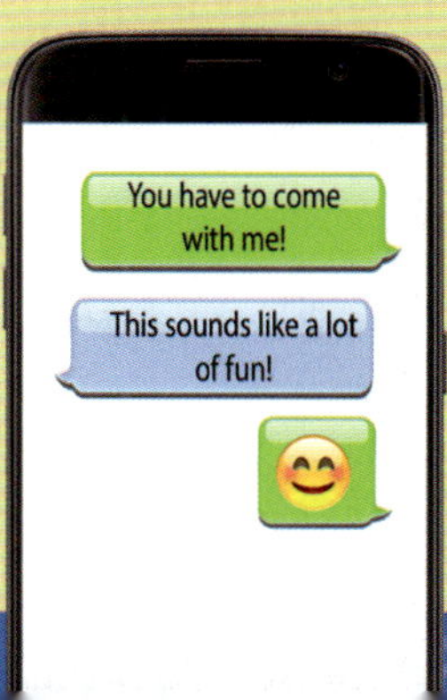

The Goal of Communication

The goal of any kind of communication is to share your message and have it be clearly understood. The goal is also to receive a response. But was your message understood? The best way to find out is to listen to the feedback you get.

Effective Communication

Did the other person do as you asked?

Did the other person answer your question?

Did the other person laugh at your joke?

Ineffective Communication

Or did they ask you to repeat what you said?

Or did they reply with another question?

Or did they seem confused?

It can be frustrating when people don't understand your message. But if they don't, then you are probably not communicating effectively. When this happens, think about what you can do to help others understand you. Can you say your message another way or use a different tool to share it?

Digital Communication

You can use digital **media** to communicate effectively. Digital tools can help you share your message in different ways—such as **verbal**, written, **visual**, or through videos. The tool you use will depend on the type of message. A list of instructions will probably need to be written down—and maybe helped with images that show each step. A comedy routine needs to be shared verbally—and maybe with video, too. Examine the chart below. Which digital tools are right for your messages?

Your Digital Choices	Written Word	Spoken Word	Images	Video
SMARTPHONE	✓	✓	✓	✓
EMAIL	✓		✓	✓
SLIDESHOW	✓	✓	✓	✓
SOCIAL MEDIA	✓	✓	✓	✓
BLOG	✓		✓	✓
PODCAST		✓		
WIKI	✓		✓	✓

Lifelong Digital Citizen

You are a digital citizen. You have been one your entire life. With a digital device you can communicate with people all around the world in seconds. Because you live in a digital world, you can travel the world without leaving home. You are part of a global community of digital technology users.

What does it mean to be a citizen?

You are a citizen of the place where you are born. The places in which you are a citizen describe your relationship to others in the world. Being a citizen gives you **rights** and **privileges**—but it also gives you duties. In the digital world, you have the duty to interact safely, communicate positively with others, and contribute your creativity.

Digital Tools and the Law

If you are 13 or older, you can sign up for websites or digital tools, such as apps, by yourself. You can start your own blog. You can send email. You can chat on video.

Why do you need to be 13? The Child Online Privacy Protection Act (COPPA) is a law in the United States that protects young people online. Companies online cannot collect any information about people under 13. If you are under 13, you will need an adult to help you communicate using digital tools.

The Golden Rule

Treat others the way you want to be treated. That's the Golden Rule. It's a rule you should follow as a digital citizen, too.

When you surf online, send direct messages on Instagram, or post videos on YouTube, you leave a digital footprint. This is a record of all your digital activity. Once you share something in the digital world, you lose control of where it goes. You may go back and delete it, but you can't make everyone else do that. Whoever you shared it with can save a copy and share it too. So it's important to think about your online image. The goal is to be a positive influence in the digital commnunity.

Becoming a positive influence as a digital citizen is a lifelong process. But you can get started by learning to choose and use digital tools that allow you to communicate clearly and positively with others. Being a digital citizen isn't only about being safe online. It is being empowered to use digital tools to contribute positively to the global digital community. You are a lifelong digital citizen!

Email

Email is the mail that you send with electronic equipment, such as on a smartphone or computer. Email is a digital tool you can use to communicate. It is a form of written communication that can be used for many purposes: from informing someone about an upcoming event to entertaining them with funny stories.

Your Electronic Mailbox

Email travels from one digital device to another. It is sent from one electronic mailbox to another electronic mailbox. Email can send messages between two people only. They can be near each other or far away. An email can provide you with an instant message from your grandmother who lives in another country. Email also allows people to send messages to many people at once. Your coach can send an email about the next practice to everyone on your team at the same time.

An Email is an Electronic Letter

When you write a letter on paper, it has five parts:

1. Heading
2. Greeting
3. Body
4. Closing
5. Signature

Heading

In a letter written on paper, the heading has the date and an address at the top. In an email, the heading is in the subject line. The subject line tells the receiver what is in the email. The date and time of the email will also be shown—either at the top or bottom.

Greeting

The greeting is next. How will you greet the person reading your email? If you are sending an email to a friend, you can use their name here. If you are sending an email to an adult, use their title instead (Mr., Mrs., Ms., and Miss) just like you would at school.

New Message

To Wondering what goes here? Turn the page. Cc Bcc

Subject Basketball practice at 2 today

Today 07:38 AM

Hello J.V. Team!

Just a reminder that basketball practice is at 2:00 today because of early release. We'll go back to our regular 3:00 practice on Friday.

See you there,

Coach Clark

Body

The body of the email is where you write what you want to say. Just like a letter on paper, using punctuation helps your reader understand what you are saying. Start a new sentence for each idea you have. Start a new paragraph when you start writing about a new topic.

Closing

After you have shared all of your ideas, say goodbye. Write a short closing and add a comma.

Signature

The last thing to add is your signature. Write your name at the bottom of your email.

Sending Email

Just like other forms of communication, email works two ways. You can be the sender or the receiver. When you receive an email, you can write back. Just click the word Reply, and a new email message will open.

Of course, you don't have to wait for an email to come in before you send your own email. You can send the first email, too. Click the word New or Compose at the top of the screen to open a new email.

Address Line

Write the name of the person you want to email on this line. If they are already saved as a contact in your address book, their name will come up right away. The **software** will fill in the name and the email address automatically. If you don't have the person in your address book yet, you can type their email address in the address line. After they send you a reply, you can click on their name and add them to the contacts in your address book.

CC

The address line also has the letters, CC. This stands for "carbon copy." Long ago you had to place **carbon paper** under a sheet of paper to make two copies at one time. The sheet of paper under the carbon paper was called the carbon copy.

To send a copy of your letter to another person, click on the CC. Then type the second person's name or email address.

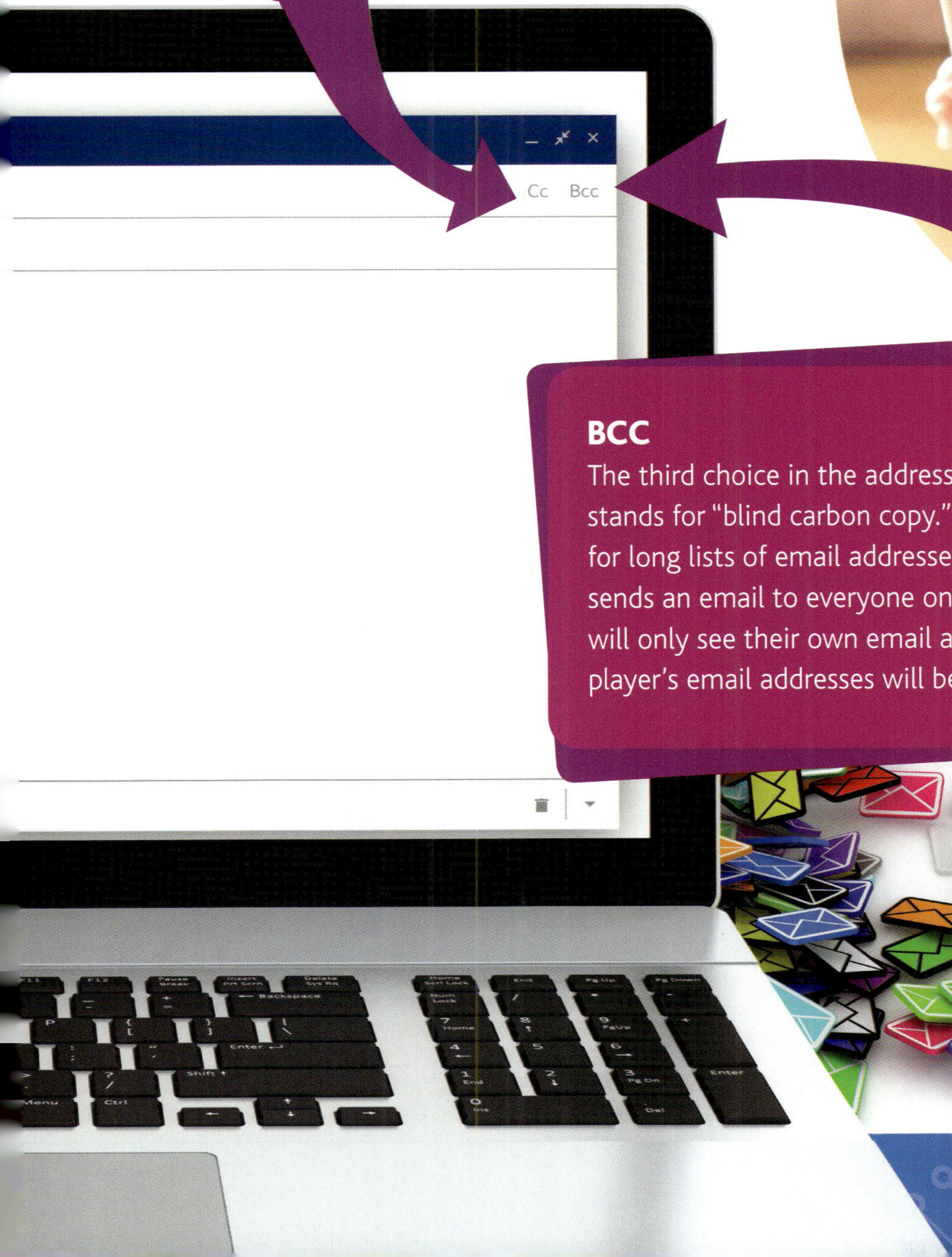

BCC

The third choice in the address line is BCC. That stands for "blind carbon copy." This is the best choice for long lists of email addresses. When the coach sends an email to everyone on the team, each player will only see their own email address. The other player's email addresses will be invisible.

Clear Communication

Electronic communication is fast and easy, but it can be tricky. When you talk to someone, you can see if the other person doesn't understand you. When you send an email, you are not there.

How can you make sure that the other person understands your email? Start with the subject line.

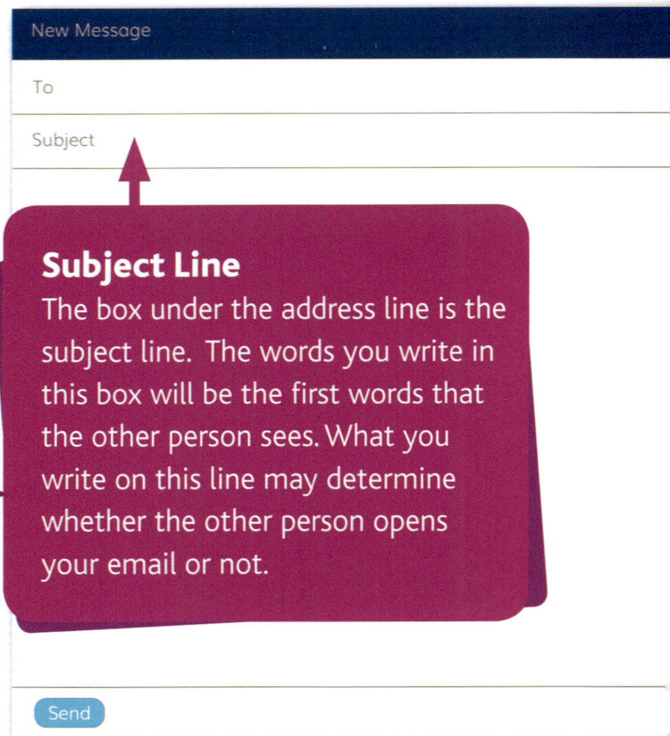

Subject Line
The box under the address line is the subject line. The words you write in this box will be the first words that the other person sees. What you write on this line may determine whether the other person opens your email or not.

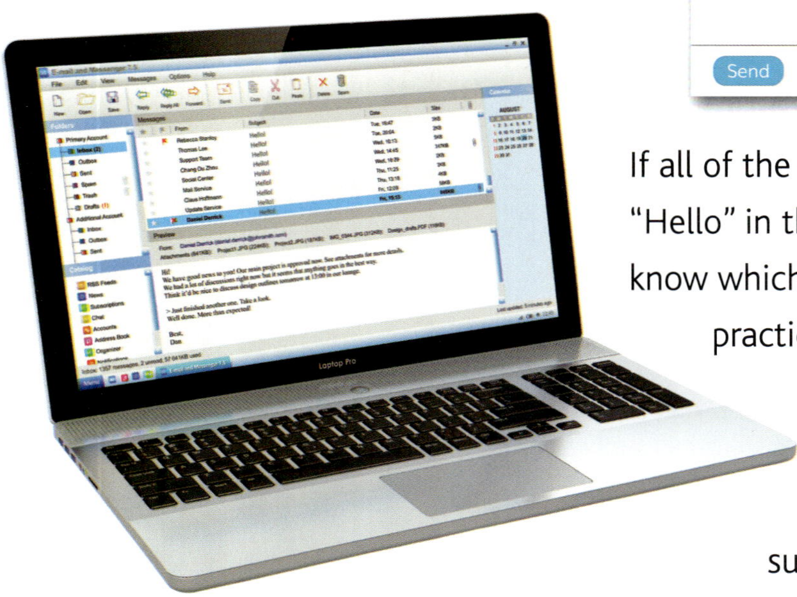

If all of the emails in your inbox said "Hello" in the subject line, how would you know which one was about basketball practice? On the other hand, if the subject line says "Basketball practice at 2 today", you could find it right away. The subject was clear.

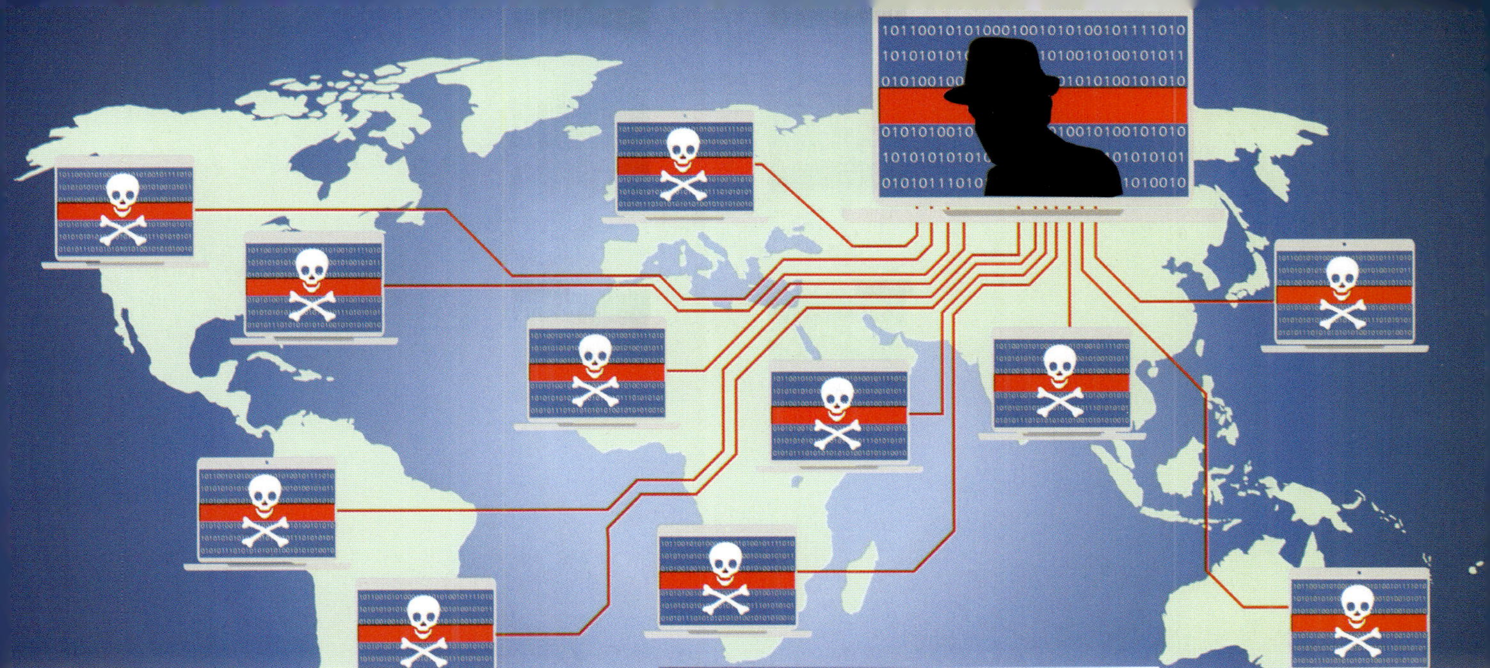

Keep your device safe by only opening emails from people you know, and choosing not to click on unknown links.

Safe Email Practices

Did you know that robots can send email? Robots that work on the Internet are called bots. These robots do the same thing over and over.

If you get an email from someone you don't know, it could be sent by a bot. Some people use bots to send **viruses**. The viruses could damage your computer or allow a **hacker** to access your information. Some viruses start working when you open the bot's email. Others start when you click on a link in an email. These could start a **malware program** which could take over your device, allowing a hacker to control it.

Blogging

A blog is a website that acts as an online journal. You can reach a lot of people by blogging! They are usually **public**—but you can also choose who views your blog on some sites. You can use a blog to share your thoughts. You can also share images and videos on a blog. Vlogs are blogs done entirely using video. Vloggers record their thoughts instead of writing them down.

You can blog at home or you can blog at school. If you want to blog from home, Blogger and WordPress are two popular (and free) choices. Blogger is a Google app. If you have a free Gmail account, you can also start your own blog.

WordPress is another popular blogging platform. The **code** used in WordPress blogs is **open-source**. That means it is created by coders all around the world—and is free to use.

School Blogs

Schools have been using Edublogs since 2005. If your teacher signs up for a free account, you can blog at school, too! Edublogs are a special type of WordPress blog.

School blogs usually have student blogs linked to the teacher's blog. Everyone in the class has a blog that is linked to the teacher's blog. For a school blog, the teacher will give you a different task each time. These tasks, called blog challenges, will show you how to try different things.

DIGITAL DYNAMO

SHIRLEY'S 6TH GRADE

In 2015, a sixth-grade class won a group blogging award from Edublogs. How did they do it? Each student had a blog linked to the class blog. The students participated in blogging challenges during the entire school year.

For one challenge, the class blogged with three other schools from around the world. When four schools blog together, it is called quadblogging. For this challenge, students from schools around the world get to know one another by visiting each other's blogs. The students from each school added comments on the other school's blog.

TECH TIP

One of the goals of quadblogging is to add "quality" comments. What is a quality comment? Use the THINK **acronym** to help you decide. Before you click the Publish button, look at what you wrote. Is it:

T: Is it true?
H: Is it helpful?
I: Is it inspiring?
N: Is it necessary?
K: Is it kind?

Starting Your Own Blog

The first thing to do when you create your blog is to choose a **template**. Every blog platform has numerous templates to use. Some templates have one wide panel in the middle with a narrow sidebar panel on the left or the right. Others have two or three wide panels side by side. Choose the one that you like best.

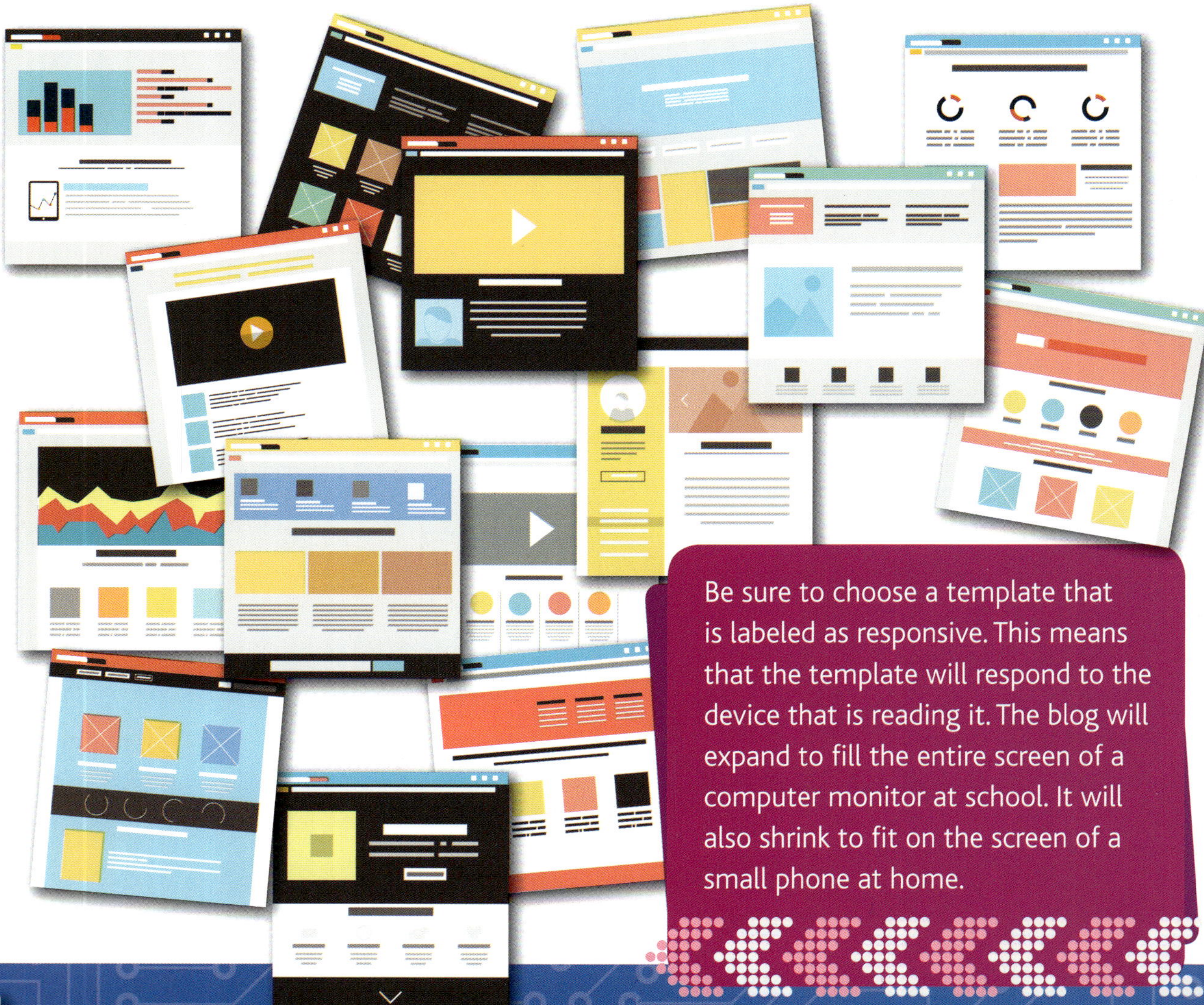

Be sure to choose a template that is labeled as responsive. This means that the template will respond to the device that is reading it. The blog will expand to fill the entire screen of a computer monitor at school. It will also shrink to fit on the screen of a small phone at home.

Name Your Blog

The first thing to do after you create your blog is to give it a name. Most school blogs use only the student's first name. This serves two purposes. Using only your first name will protect your privacy. It also helps your family find your blog when they want to read it.

Add a Tagline

After you name your blog, give it a tagline. This one-line description of your blog will explain a bit more about you and what you want to blog about.

Music is my happy place.

DIGITAL DYNAMO

MR. GEIMAN'S UNBOUNDED CLASSROOM

The students in Mr. Geiman's fourth grade class also won a group award from Edublogs in 2015. Four individual students were also nominated for individual awards! Each of these students used their own name in the blog title. They also added a tagline that showed their personality.

Moses named his blog, Moses's Blog. His tagline said: "In order to succeed, we must first believe that we can." Abby named her blog, Abby's Authentic Blog. Her tagline said: "Be like a pineapple . . . stand tall, wear a crown, and be sweet on the inside!" At the end of the tagline, Abby added a happy face. What blog tagline would you use to represent your personality?

Pages and Posts

Pages and Posts

Adding content to your blog is the next step. There are two ways to share your thoughts and images on a blog. You can make a page, or you can create a post. So what is the difference?

Blog Pages

A blog page is used for basic information. Most blogs have an About page and a Contact page. For a school blog, the teacher will add a page that outlines the rules of the blog.

Your blog will likely show the name of the pages you make in a menu bar at the top, bottom, or side. To go to a page, your visitor will click on the words and the page will open. You can choose the order in which the pages are displayed.

Unlike blog posts, the information on pages does not change or update often. So readers won't see dates and times on those pages.

Blog Posts

Blog posts usually show up in one place, unless you decide to give the posts separate pages. Usually, blogs have a menu option to go to the post page.

The blog posts are your "entries." They usually read from newest to oldest. Whenever you add a new post, it appears on the top of your blog. To see the old ones, you have to scroll down.

Each new blog post you write will show you as the author. It will also show the time and date you published it.

TECH TIP

You can spice up your posts with images and videos. But remember that each time you use an image or video that is not your own, you have to give **credit**, or say where it came from and who made it.

How do you think adding images and videos to your blog posts changes how others will understand your message?

Telling a Story

Traditionally, storytelling was a verbal form of communication. Stories were usually shared in person, as a form of entertainment. But today, you can use words and images to tell stories on digital devices. You can tell stories from your imagination. Or you can share stories that are **representations** of your life. Listening to others' stories is a wonderful way to learn about people's lives in different places around the world.

DIGITAL DYNAMO

Milani's Ballet Blog

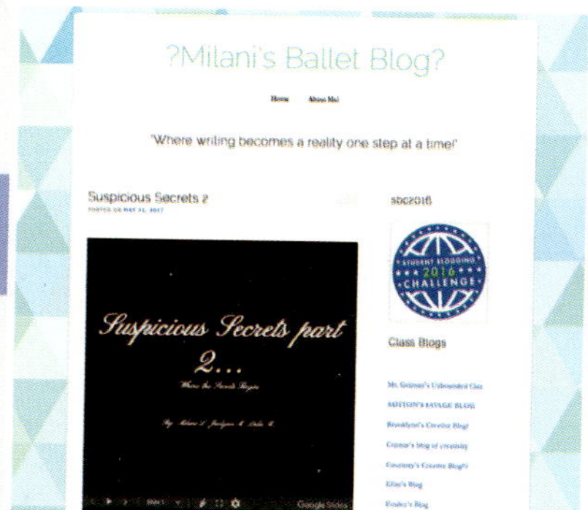

Milani started blogging in the fourth grade. She uses Google Slides to tell stories with words and images in her blog posts. One story was told in four parts or episodes. Each episode in the story was a new blog post with a new slide deck. This strategy kept her readers coming back for more!

Tell a Story with Words and Images

Tell a story with words and images like Milani did. Borrow an idea from a favorite book and write your own version. Or write an original story.

TECH TIP

Choose a Google Slides template you like and upload your images. Then add the text and think about the **transitions**. How long do you want each slide to show on screen? Drag the slider to set the time for each slide.

STEP 1

Make a simple storyboard first. Draw eight squares on a sheet of paper. Write the name of the story in the first square. Then add your own name. Now you have a title and an author.

STEP 2

What will you write in the other seven squares? Think of two characters and what they could say to one another. Or, begin with the setting and think of a place where something could happen. Seven squares is just enough room for a short scene. What could happen? Make notes on your storyboard.

STEP 3

It can be challenging to find images of the characters and setting you envision. You might have to make some changes along the way! But that is part of the process. Remember to give credit if you use an image taken by someone else.

STEP 4

Place an image of the story setting on a few of your slides. Then write the words in your story. You can show **dialogue** by writing the character's name in capital letters, then their speech after it.

STEP 5

If your story grows longer than eight slides, take a page from Milani's book. Write "To Be Continued" on the last slide, and then finish the story in another episode.

Visual Communication

As the saying, goes, a picture is worth a thousand words. Sometimes a picture is one of the best ways to communicate.

Make a Photo Gallery

Use pictures to send a clear message. On a blog or on social media, upload four photos that describe you. You can take the photos yourself, or you can find them online. The challenge is to include images that show your interests without showing any faces. Then, ask friends and family if they get your visual message!

DIGITAL DYNAMO

Rayne's Blog

In December 2015, Rayne's Blog was one of five selected for the Best Student Blog. He used many visual communication tools to show his ideas, making his blog stand out.

TECH TIP

With photo gallery software code, your blog can organize your photos into a grid that is easy to see. If you are blogging on WordPress, you can turn on the gallery setting in the Jetpack plugin. For Blogger, you can download a free photo gallery widget.

Create an Infographic

Another project that Rayne did was to create an **infographic**. Words and images come together in an infographic to share information. Most infographics use multiple images. The amount of words is kept to a minimum. The words are there to support the images.

Begin with a design software program, such as Canva. Log in online and select the infographic template. A new screen will open. Choose one of the examples in the left sidebar. After you select one, the design will move to the right. Now you can change whatever you want! You can change the images, the words, the fonts, and the colors. After you finish, give the design a name and download it.

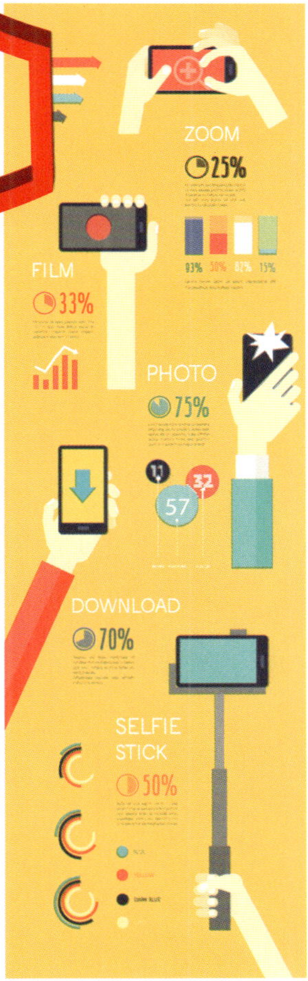

TECH TIP

You can use Canva on your device without downloading an app. Just make a free account and log in online. If your school has a Piktochart account, you can use that to make an infographic, too. Both software programs have libraries of graphics and fonts for you to choose in the sidebar on the left.

Overcoming Communication Roadblocks

It might seem easy to communicate with all of these digital tools at your fingertips. But that's not always the case. Sometimes, there are communication roadblocks. Someone may not understand your message. People could use digital tools to send hurtful messages. Or there could be barriers such as language differences. Luckily, there are digital tools to help overcome barriers, too.

DIGITAL DYNAMO

Amanda Moore

Being a new student at school is always a challenge. After Rafael Anaya started school, he always sat alone at lunch. Amanda Moore didn't think that was right. But he spoke only Spanish and she spoke only English. So Amanda used a Google Translate app on her phone to translate English words to Spanish. Amanda wrote down the words and took the note to school. The note asked Rafael to sit with her at lunch. Their story went viral and was reported around the country. A digital tool helped two students break the language barrier.

TECH TIP

With the Google Translate app, you can translate text, handwriting, photos, and speech in over 100 languages. You can also use it on your computer to translate pages you read on the Internet.

Digital Communication and You

Negative news and messages online can spread quickly—but you can use digital communication to be a positive influence in the global digital community. Practice the Golden Rule, and share safe and meaningful messages with others. Remember that building your digital communication skills is an ongoing process! You are a lifelong digital learner.

TECH TIP

#IAmAWitness

Cyberbulling is an issue that has come along with the advancement of digital technology. When hurtful messages go directly to someone's digital device, they can feel like they can't escape the bullying. As digital citizens, we have a responsibility to stand against cyberbullying.

You can use the #IAmAWitness eye emoji to support people being bullied online. When you see cyberbullying happening, send the person being bullied a message with the emoji to let them know that you witnessed what happened. This will help them feel that they have support. Then stop the hate by changing the conversation. Say something positive to your friend and stand against cyberbullying.

Glossary

acronym A word formed from the first letters of a set of different words

app A mobile program or application that is downloaded to a device

carbon paper Thin paper that is coated in carbon, and used to make copies of typed documents. Carbon is a dark material formed after something is burned, such as charcoal

code A set of symbols that give directions to the software

communicate To share thoughts, ideas, and feelings

credit To publicly acknowledge someone in the creation of a work

cyberbullying Bullying through electronic communication

dialogue Conversation between two or more people, as written in a script or story

digital Describing something characterized by electronic and computerized technology

digital citizen A person who uses digital technology

digital community People who interact through the Internet or digital platforms

hacker A person who illegally accesses data on computers

infographic A visual image such as a chart or diagram that represents information or data

malware programs Any software that harms a computer system

media A means of communication, such as the Internet

open-source Describes software for which the original code is freely available

podcast A series of audio files that others listen to

privileges Advantages given to certain people

public Shared in open view, or for all people

slide deck A group of slides in a presentation

software The program used to give directions to a digital device

representation A description or depiction of someone or something

rights The things that people are legally able to do or have

template An electronic file with a customized form to fill in

transitions The changes from one state to another

verbal Relating to spoken words

viruses Pieces of code that can copy themselves and harm computer systems

visual Relating to sight

wiki A website that allows anyone to add, delete, or revise content

Learning More

Websites

https://www.canva.com/create/infographics/
Use this free drag-and-drop infographic creator online.

http://help.edublogs.org/image-gallery/
Follow the directions on this Edublogs Support page to add an image gallery to your blog. Don't have an EduBlog account? Ask your teacher about setting one up!

https://www.google.com/slides/about/
Master the art of Google Slides and learn how to use it for all of your digital devices. Then get started on telling your stories!

http://iwitnessbullying.org/how-to-use-the-eye
Learn how to use the #IAmAWitness eye emoji and join other eye witnesses when you see cyberbullying.

Books

Anniss, Matthew. *Create Your Own Web Site or Blog*. Heinemann-Raintree. 2017.

Gifford, Clive. *Super Social Media and Awesome Online Safety.* Crabtree Publishing Company. 2018.

Raum, Elizabeth. *Social Media Savvy: Facts and Figures About Selfies, Smartphones, and Standing Out*. Capstone Press. 2018.

Index

addresses 13, 14, 15, 16
apps 5, 10, 18, 27, 28, 29
Blogger 18, 27
blogs 10, 18-23, 24, 26
pages 22, 23
posts 22, 23, 24
blind carbon copy 15
body 13
bots 17
Canva 27
carbon copy 15
challenges 18, 19, 26, 28
Child Online Privacy Protection Act (COPPA) 10
closing 13
code 18, 27
communication
  face to face 5, 7
  reasons for 7
  verbal 9, 24-25, 28
  visual 9, 26-27
  written 9, 12-13
communication barriers 28
computers 12, 17, 20, 29
credit 23, 25
cyberbullying 29
dialogue 25
digital citizen 5, 10-11, 29
digital community 5, 11, 29
digital technology 5, 10, 29
Edublogs 18, 19, 21
emails 10, 12-17
emojis 5, 29
Facetime 5
feedback 6, 8
fonts 27
Gmail 18
goals 8, 11, 19
Golden Rule 11
Google 18, 25
Google Slides 24, 25
Google Translate 28, 29
hackers 17
#**I**AmAWitness 29
influence 11, 29
infographics 27
Instagram 5, 11
Internet 27, 29
languages 28, 29
malware 17
media 9
messages 6, 8-9, 11, 12, 14, 23, 26, 28, 29
payphones 4
photo galleries 26-27
photos 5, 26, 27, 29
platforms 8, 20
privilege 10
publishing 19, 23
punctuation 13
quadblogging 19
receivers 6, 8, 13, 14
representations 21, 24
rights 10
safety 5, 20, 11, 17, 29
senders 6, 14, 17
sharing 4, 5, 6, 8, 9, 11, 13, 18, 22, 24, 27, 29
signatures 13
Skype 5
slide deck 24
slides 25
smartphones 5, 6, 12
Snapchat 5
social media 26
software 14, 27
stories 12, 24-25, 28
storyboards 25
subject line 13, 16
taglines 21
templates 20, 25, 27
text messages 5, 6
THINK acronym 19
topics 13
transitions 25
videos 5, 9, 10, 11, 18, 23
viruses 17
vlogs 18
websites 10, 18
WordPress 18, 27

About the Author

Anastasia Suen is the author of more than 300 books for children, teens, and adults. For more than 20 years, she has used digital tools to mentor writers and communicate with students, teachers, librarians, and editors.